P

By

On the Occasion of

Date

WHY DIDN'T I THINK OF THAT?

2001 Original Proverbs for Life and Faith

Raymond P. Brunk

BARBOUR
PUBLISHING, INC.
Uhrichsville, Ohio

Although we are a part of all whom we have met, the author has not knowingly quoted from any other sources.

© 2000 by Raymond Brunk

ISBN 1-57748-798-2

Published by Barbour Publishing, Inc., P. O. Box 719, Uhrichsville, Ohio 44683 http://www.barbourbooks.com

 Member of the
Evangelical Christian
Publishers Association

Printed in the United States of America.

DEDICATION

This book is dedicated to my wife, Reba.
My love for you is strong and continues
to be strengthened and will be fully realized
in our eternal life together.

CONTENTS

FOREWORD

With crispness and skill, the author brings big subjects into focus in the continuing pursuit of improving one's own life and in understanding and appreciating other people.

You will find *Why Didn't I Think of That?* a most unique and inspiring book. It is not to be hurried through in one reading, but to be used bit by bit and time after time for meditation and soul enrichment. Pick it up and read one or more of the "proverbs." They are stimulating; you will think deeply, see places for personal improvement, smile, and sometimes weep. They are for quiet meditation or for discussion, some to go to sleep on, and some to awaken to, but all to grow on.

Why Didn't I Think of That? is designed to stimulate and bring one's thoughts out of a possible state of indifference and inactivity to one of heaven-sent enrichment and insight.

Raymond P. Brunk was brought up in a Christian home of high ideals. As a layman, he founded a gospel tract and cassette ministry in 1980. This ministry is based on the author's series of tracts based on the sayings of Jesus.

In the early years, the demand for these

materials rose rapidly. During this time, other church laymen who were supportive became involved in organizing Gospel Sunrise, Inc., of which Raymond P. Brunk is president. In addition, Mr. Brunk is self-employed and is a Bible teacher in the church and in institutional homes. Gospel Sunrise now distributes millions of tracts and tens of thousands of cassette tapes worldwide annually.

The author's prayer, "Lord, save a soul through me," is typical of his fervent zeal for soul winning. As a layman, he believes that each Christian has his part to do in kingdom work, and that one does not need to be someone special. It is a task for everyone.

In today's world, life for many is hurried and often complicated, with days filled with many activities and personal pursuits, leaving little time for meditation. It seems everyone is looking for shortcuts in the daily routine of life. Sometimes it takes only a sentence, a word or a phrase to bring courage and hope in times of tension or distress. It is then that one may realize the important and satisfying place of communicating with one's own self and with God.

With a marked, godly subtlety, the author challenges each reader to meditation and serious thinking. As the great churchman A. W. Tozer has said, "God and man and their relation to each other is what matters in the world." And this book is written to enhance that way of life.

KATIE FLORENCE SHANK

ADVERSARY

Be sure you understand your
adversary's question before responding.

Do not allow good people to
become your enemies.

Enemies come only in one size.

If your enemy throws salt at you and it burns,
then you'll know where your sore places are.

Never make enemies.
They make themselves.

Place yourself on the scale
before weighing your enemy.

Prevent anyone from becoming your enemy.

Suppose your adversary
died in your verbal combat.

The devil is your only mortal enemy.

There are no small enemies.

You cannot determine who will dislike you,
but you are responsible for
your response to them.

Your adversary may oppose you because he
unwittingly understands you.

Your enemy could be your best teacher.

Your strengths may be
your accuser's weaknesses.

ANGER

A person is in bad company when
he is beside himself with rage.

An opinion formed in anger is long lasting.

Anger and bad temper may be strangers.

Anger and despair are very close kin.

Anger causes memory loss.

Anger is one of society's greatest motivations.

Anger leads to argument.

Anger may be a habit.

Anger often stems from sorrow.

Answering an angry word is unnecessary.

Argument is a child of anger.

Delay is an antidote for anger.

Envy and anger feed each other.

Hiding anger is stressful.

How can one be angry at a child?

How long can one burn with anger
and not be consumed?

How many degrees of anger are there?

If you are too angry to pray, you are too angry.

Live so the angry person is mystified.

Opinions formed in anger are dangerous.

Secret anger can consume one
from the inside out.

Some people are angered when
an argument is avoided.

Staying calm takes the wind out of
an angry man's sails.

The aggressor's anger may follow his attack.

The mean person tortures himself
in his effort to hurt others.

The person who is angry with you may expect
you to be impressed with his anger.

*The quickest way to self-hatred
is a bad temper.*

When a person is angry, he may speak
thoughts he previously held secret.

When angry,
a person may say more than he knows.

When angry, count "one, two, three,"
then behave yourself.

When writing a letter in anger,
allow time to destroy it.

You can't shake hands with a clenched fist.

BELIEFS

A person's beliefs determine
his accomplishments.

A belief is a command to action.

An atheist has a very personal reason
to deny God.

An atheist is a man with his eyes closed
complaining that he cannot see.

An atheist is one who whistles in the dark
of his own making.

An atheist may speak more about God
than the local pastor.

Are your convictions worth dying for?

Belief requires action.

Believe carefully.

*Believe in God,
not someone's interpretation of Him.*

Believe what you wish
but bear the consequences.

Even the atheist plants a seed
and waits for God to make it grow.

Every man craves a woman who
will believe in him.

Freedom of belief is the freedom to be wrong.

If you don't want to think,
believe everything.

The true scientist cannot be an atheist.

There is an originality in belief as well as in
creativity.

Too many people believe more
than they know.

Too many people have
no basis for their beliefs.

You cannot believe what you hold to be
improbable.

*You must believe the gospel
before you can live it.*

THE BIBLE

An atheist attempts to misuse Scripture to
prove it doesn't mean what it says.

An effective Bible scholar puts
the Scriptures to practical use.

As no other book, the Bible exalts truth.

If you have read the Bible with sincerity,
you know it is God's Word for all mankind.

Life is unexplainable without
the knowledge of the Bible.

Most preaching modifies the Holy Scriptures.

Our attitude toward the first sentence of the
Bible determines our attitude toward the rest.

The Bible has inspired more books than any other book.

The Bible tells people what to do
and the newspaper tells what they did.

The Bible was not written by a committee.

The person who knows the Bible
will not reject it.

The sincere believer is
delighted with biblical truths.

Too many people are challenged by the Bible,
but unchanged.

Too often, folks read the Bible to confirm
their opinions.

CHANGE

After prayer changes me,
then I change things.

Despair is hope changed from green to black.

It is not possible to change the past,
but you may correct it.

*Nothing can bring progress
except change.*

Reputation changes rapidly.
Character alters slowly.

Some people are so rigid that
they cannot change.

The beginning may be faulty,
but our lives can change course
for a glorious ending.

The person who never changes his mind
is a weakling.

The true observer sees himself in others—
and improves himself.

*Too many people
want to change everything.*

With age, the music of life
can change to a minor key.

CHRISTIAN LIFE

A Christian can rise from failure.

A Christian is a true futurist.

*A Christian is amazed
by what God's grace can do.*

A Christian with his attention attached to
the affairs within the church turns
his back on those without.

A church's discipline should enrich,
not condemn.

Am I living as I wish to be remembered?

As a Christian,
you are a preacher and you are a sermon.

Be sure your claim to be a Christian
can be verified.

Christian faith requires action.

Christian graces are revealed in humanly
impossible circumstances.

Christian joy comes from the knowledge of
God, not circumstances.

Christian maturity comes through
obedience to God.

Christian mission is God's chain letter.

Christianity expands not only
the intellect but the heart.

Christianity has its traitors.

Christianity is natural law.

Christianity is growth; atheism is death.

Christianity is not picking thorns
and ignoring roses.

Christianity is simple and profound.

Christianity is the epitome of humanity.

Christianity is the fruition of Judaism.

Christianity is the medicine that
works for everybody.

Christianity was not intended to be
a formal religion.

Christians are tall enough to gaze above
the present trouble to the horizon beyond.

Christians have God's peace.

Christians light the path for others.

Christians should out-live, out-love
and out-laugh everyone.

Conscious Christian service loses its blessing.

Don't merely stand for the Christian faith; walk.

Dragging your cross is much harder
than carrying it.

Family was the first form of the church.

God is the Christian's armor.

Has the message of Jesus been thwarted
more by His Church or by the world?

If you are a Christian, live in big letters.

In some churches, the great awakening occurs
at the end of the service.

Judas would feel at home in many churches.

*Let your Christian heart
be your tabernacle.*

Love the preacher who speaks for your good.

Many Christians attempt to follow
themselves in Jesus' name.

Many Christians cannot see God
unless He aligns with their bias.

Many Christians glitter, but few glow.

Neither the church nor the state profits from their union.

No one can out-give a Christian.

Often the mature Christian walks alone.

One believer is not a church.

Only the active Christian is fully at rest.

Preaching instructs and reminds.

Relax and enjoy God.

*Religion is composed of promises.
Only Christianity is true.*

Restlessness is the fruit of human philosophy.

Rest is the fruit of Christ.

The basis of the Christian life is
repentance toward God.

The Christian does not experience
a smooth cross.

The Christian does not judge
the future by the past.

The Christian faith magnifies goodness.

The Christian life focuses on Jesus.

The Christian never knows when he is dead
because he lives forever.

The Christian should never be a pessimist.

The Christian stands,
hands outstretched to God and the world.

The Christian's cross must be
as real as a gallows.

The church does not react to the world;
it confronts it.

The church that keeps the gospel from the
world also keeps it from themselves.

The cross is the line of demarcation.

The devil is stymied by
a happy and victorious Christian.

The effective Christian is a priest.

*The happy Christian radiates
messages of hope.*

The leaders of God's people
lead by example more than by word.

The medical practitioner
seeks to heal the body.
The Christian worker strives to cure the soul.

The poor man is more of a stranger in
this world than is a rich Christian.

The sinner lives and then dies.
The Christian lives and then lives again.

The true Christian lives like one.

The world ignores many Christians because
it doesn't see them as being different.

The world is startled to see
Christianity practiced.

There is no greater discord than
perverted Christianity.

*To be a child of God
is life's highest calling.*

To the Christian,
life's detours can be the most fruitful.

Too many Christians are
guilty of spiritual treason.

When a Christian grows, he glows.

When we rightly carry our cross,
other cross-bearing Christians feel
no interference.

Would revival occur if
churches taxed hypocrisy?

Conscience

A clear conscience is a marvelous weapon
in the battle for truth.

A guilty conscience abhors solitude.

A person who is fighting guilt
takes on all comers.

Conscience will forgive more quickly
than memory.

Does truth witness for or against you?

Educate your conscience truthfully,
then guard it carefully;
it is the only one you will ever have.

Guilt is a lion tearing with dull teeth.

People disobey their consciences,
but few reject them.

Many people speak of a "clear conscience"
while very few mention a partly cloudy one.

Moral conditioning requires intensive training.

Never let your conscience become your enemy.

To the guilty, the world has big eyes.

Too often it's your accuser's self-interest
and not his conscience that is bothering him.

We must be courageous
even when there is no battle.

You cannot accuse your conscience.

Your conscience is your character.

Your critics may have
nothing against you personally;
you just may be upsetting
their guilty consciences.

*Your genius is no stronger
than your conscience.*

COURAGE

Are you strong enough to hold your tongue?

Courage is fear that dares to act.

Courage is portrayed by virtue, not by force.

Courage walks with hope.

Courageous people usually stand alone.

Cowards exaggerate.

Does it take courage to do wrong?

Hope and courage are relatives.

Hope enlarges courage.

Hope exalts courage.

I know it takes strength to change,
but when I am wrong, dear God,
please give me that courage.

Is it courage if you are not afraid?

It is better to be praised for courage
than for beauty.

It takes no courage to react.

Some courageous folks are also fools.

Survival promotes courage.

The courage to do right is the greatest virtue.

The most courageous person is one who
always does what is right.

CREATIVITY

A sanctified imagination is a priceless gem.

*Commanded thoughts
stunt creativity.*

Creativity and poverty don't know each other.

Desires fuel the mind.

False censure by another destroys
personal creativity.

One becomes selfish when
he has nothing creative to offer.

Praise promotes creativity.

The best is known by its difficulty to achieve.

The narrow mind habitually imprisons
a creative thought.

When an inspired idea
crashes into you,
hold it close; keep it warm;
let it grow.

Words are raw material;
build with them carefully.

CRITICISM

A critic with a vocabulary can say good things.

A new way does not criticize the old.

Can it be that a critic simply cannot understand?

Critics know where you hurt.

Critics often try to cut you down to their size.

Do you find it difficult to be a silent critic?

Don't allow your opposition to make
your just criticism appear cynical.

Don't you wish you had the influence your
critics think you have?

Have my emotions been bruised most
by friends or by critics?

*Ignore your critics at eventide,
for they are weary, too.*

Look for a better way than criticism.

Most failures criticize others' success.

No one criticizes a candle's light.

Nothing prompts criticism like excellence.

Since your critics cannot equal you,
they attack you.

Success is difficult for critics.

Take it easy on your critics—
they may be trying to be as good as you are.

The accused may sleep better than his critic.

The activist thrills when his critics disagree.

The critic seldom elevates himself
to the level of his subject.

The realist is more criticized than the optimist.

Those who qualify to criticize others often don't.

*Virtue may be lost when
good is criticized.*

You may need to lower your eyes
to look your critic in the eye.

DEATH

A dead person is silent.
Memories speak volumes.

A graveyard speaks soberly.

Are funerals the pretty side of death?

At death,
the atheist receives the ultimate surprise.

Be like nature—die in bright colors.

Death calls not by character.

Death forsakes no one.

Death is necessary for the
redemption of our bodies.

Death keeps its secrets.

*Do not ignore death,
but look through it to eternal life.*

Dollar marks aren't found on tombstones.

Don't trust your doctor too much.
Death will overtake him, too.

Every writer has a deadline: his death.

Farewells are symbolic of death.

In death, the curtain is lifted after the event.

Is there anyone whose emotions
are not moved by death?

Life gives us continuous reminders of death.

Many fear life because they fear death.

Many people do not understand
the purpose of life until they face death.

*Many people fear death because
it may terminate incomplete lives.*

Many who dislike life feel the same about death.

Many people use friends
as a hedge against death.

My death is coming to me; I shall not go to it.

My view of life is based on my view of death.

No matter how great a man may be,
he requires little space in death.

No one repents of suicide.

Sacrifice means death.

Sin should frighten more than death.

Since sleep is symbolic of death,
should you enter it without prayer?

Some fear death only when looking it in the eye.

Some fear death; others fear life.

The death angel brooks no reasoning.

The death of a good man leaves
a glow in its wake.

The grave speaks no foreign language.

The living is in time; death overtakes it.

Time is pushing you into the next world.

Too many people see death as their only future.

What is it about thunder
that reminds us of death?

When I die,
let it be a long rest after a hard day's work.

When you die, will there be a vacancy?

*Who writes the last chapter
of an autobiography?*

Yes, I am ready to die, but dear Lord,
I'm in no hurry.

Your cross means
death to your unwholesome desires.

Your view of death will temper all activities.

ENJOYMENT

An undertaker should not enjoy his work.

As one grows older,
the enjoyment of natural beauty increases.

Flowers are like human personalities,
easy to enjoy but difficult to understand.

It is difficult to help a man who
enjoys his troubles.

*It takes a very wise person
to enjoy what he has.*

Many people enjoy unhappiness;
yours as well as theirs.

People who pray only when in trouble
must enjoy the trouble.

The egoist enjoys censuring himself in public.

*The only way to enjoy freedom
is to behave yourself.*

To some people, enjoying joy is a burden.

Too many people enjoy the falseness of
their own pretenses.

We smile before we laugh.
Discretion would often stop with the smile.

Writing should tell the reader
how to enjoy life.

ENVY AND JEALOUSY

Envy and jealousy may be inherited.

Envy and jealousy bring no profit.

Envy and jealousy creep as a viper.

Envy hates the excellence that it cannot equal.

Envy is a form of sadness.

Envy is sharper than a rapier.

Envy occurs among peers.

Envy promotes envy.

Envy thrives on doubt.

Holding a grudge may give you
a spiritual hernia.

Jealousy follows strong affection.

Jealousy is seldom static.

Jealousy wounds its own feet.

Pride is a road that leads to envy.

Those people who excel need not envy.

You cannot satisfy those who envy you.

FAITH

A life of faith in God is productive.

A proof of one's faith is how he dies.

A selfish nature is an obstacle to faith.

Many people use dollars instead of faith.

Conscious faith is ineffective.

Do not be so stern and stiff in your faith
that happy joys are attributed to the devil.

Faith and generosity shake hands.

Faith and hope produce charity.

Faith and imagination are
usually at different poles.

Faith and superstition are both activities
of the mind. Only faith has evidence.

Faith ascends but doubt descends.

Faith becomes simple as death nears.

Faith can grow in a decaying society.

Faith continues to search for greater truth.

Faith in fate is fatal.

Faith in God assures no
overwhelming circumstance.

Faith in God is not a delightful fancy
but a firm reality.

Faith in God is not a leap in the dark;
it is a walk in the light.

Faith in God is proven through obedience.

Faith is not based on authority.

Faith is not won by force.

Faith leads to joy. Doubt leads to despair.

Faith reaches out; doubt clutches.

Fanatic faith is wedded to falsehood.

God is moved by the simple faith of
those who love Him.

God is not impressed with scars
but with faithfulness.

God praises not success but faithfulness.

I cannot have too much faith.

If you have faith in God, can you prove it?

It takes a soul with an active faith
to recognize God's love.

Moods may change, but not faith in God.

Our faith in God expands with experience.

*Simple faith—
is there any other kind?*

The best way to prove our faith in God
is to express it in life.

The strength of faith is in its object.

The wonder of faith comes when
it is revealed in reality.

True faith is not a hypothesis.

*You can judge your faith by
its power in you.*

FEAR

A leader does not fear cobwebs.

A leader forfeits the title when
he fears his followers.

An impartial judge is to be revered.

Cain's fear killed Abel.

Cruelty and fear are close relatives.

Dear brother, walk fearlessly but humbly.

Despair is not gray, but pitch black.

Do you obey out of fear or respect?

Don't fear the force of the opposition; it may
be the measure of their error.

Fatalism can be fatal.

Fear is generated more by ignorance
than unbelief.

Fear is painful to the soul.

Fear is the opposite of love—one is cold;
the other is warm.

Fear is the strongest emotion.

Fear the darkness of ignorance
more than a child fears a dark place.

God created fear for our protection.

He who complains of the present
fears the future.

Hope and fear keep life in balance.

If life is understood, it need not be feared.

Imagination, much more than reality,
promotes fear.

Many people fear solitude more than society.

More fears are born of prosperity
than of poverty.

More people fear justice than injustice.

Nearly everyone has a secret fear
of being misjudged.

Recognize your fears.

Some people love silence so they can
commune with their souls;
some fear it for the same reason.

That which you fear is your ruler.

*The best remedy for the fear of man
is the fear of God.*

The fear of being different
is a miserable handicap.

The fear of being hurt is
its own form of torture.

The possessor of right
should not fear a thousand enemies.

What you see as anger in others
may actually be fear.

FORGIVENESS

A brave person can forgive.

A forgiven past brings forth
a grateful benediction.

A strong person can forgive.

Forgiveness ends the quarrel.

Forgiveness removes the stinger of offense.

Forgiving the unrepentant multiplies foolery.

It is better to forgive than to forget.

Only those who have suffered
can offer true forgiveness.

The greatest adventure in life is to be forgiven.

The greatest mercy is in the word "forgiven."

Those who cannot give usually cannot forgive.

To accept forgiveness is often more
difficult than to forgive someone else.

To bear another's faults, consider your own.

Trust follows forgiveness.

FRIENDSHIP

A competitor need not be an enemy.

A friend is a light in a dark place.

A friend is friendly
regardless of circumstances.

A friend is the first person who comes in
when the whole world has gone out.

A friend makes himself vulnerable
when giving advice.

A friend with whom you have experienced
suffering claims greater loyalties.

A true friend never grows old.

A word of praise enriches two hearts.

Accepting a friend's commendation builds his self esteem.

Are you in God's circle of friends?

Are your friends attracting you into the next world?

Be sure you have enough friends to carry your casket.

Being faithful to others is the only way to please yourself.

Building a friendship takes time.

Charm finds friends while wisdom keeps them.

Do your friend a favor:
correct your own faults.

Everyone has at least one disloyal friend.

Everyone seeks a companion to please.

Everyone you meet is fighting a hard battle.
Be kind.

Fellowship is the mutual warming of souls.

Friendliness is important, even between lovers.

Friends are revealed in times of adversity.

Friends listen.

Friendship may outlive love.

Friendships grow flat when there is no
provocative interchange.

*From friends come our
greatest joys and sorrows.*

God has designed each person to need others.

Good friends are health to your soul.

I can be my best friend or worst enemy.

I paid my financial debt.
I can never pay my friendship debt.

I'd like to be a friend like you.

If a person is not friendly with himself,
he will not be to anyone else either.

In friendship, loyalty is assumed.

In providing illumination and warmth,
a candle is a wonderful friend.

Insincerity is the enemy of human relationships.

It is wise to make friends
before you need them.

It's hard to trust others
if you cannot trust yourself.

It's the good friend who says
good things behind your back.

Lovers commune silently.

Never accuse your best friends.

Never trade an old friend for a new one.

One may decide who his friends are, but he cannot control who his dear friends are.

Only God knows whether a friend will always be true.

Prosperity creates friends; adversity proves them.

Should you pick the thorns from your friends' roses?

Sleep, if you are my friend, please answer when I call.

Solitude with an intimate friend is a quiet harbor.

Surprising things occur when we befriend a rival.

Suspect affection coming from
a slight acquaintance.

The fear of being hurt is
its own form of torture.

The light of friendship is brightest when
all about us is dark.

The magnetism of your personality
attracts friends.

*The mere thought of a
true friend lifts our spirits.*

The person who trusts no one
is truly desolate.

The wonder of faith comes
when it is no longer in the unseen,
but is revealed in stark reality.

Too many people value their enemy's opinions
more than their friend's values.

Too much sympathy
can sink a wounded heart.

True friendship is the restitution that heals envy.

Warm friends dry hot tears.

When it gets dark, friends feel for each other.

Who can find a friend worth dying for?

Wise people marvel at
the number of their friends.

You are easy to think about
because you are my friend.

You decide whom you don't like.

GOD

A great person recognizes his
indebtedness to God.

A person who thinks deeply, thinks of Deity.

A person's cause for life is
based upon his concept of God.

Abundance is a part of God's nature.

Be sure your view of God is great.

Beauty points to Deity.

Do I hear the ticking clock say,
"God—God—God. . . ?"

Do you know God as patient?

Does God laugh when
men say He doesn't exist?

Does God smile when He thinks of me?

Does your life ruin
the notion that God is dead?

*Don't try to hide anything from God;
He knows it all.*

Even unbelievers are aware of a Higher Power.

God afflicts His people
to hold their attention.

God argues with no one.

God can make two snowflakes alike.

God created the earth
to meet the needs of mankind.

God did not create man as an experiment.

*God does not pay weekly;
He pays continuously.*

God does not pluck the thorns from the roses.

God doesn't speak in "thees" and "thous."

God gives benefits now; payday comes later.

God has more patience than your best friend.

God, in His love,
speaks to us at the level of our understanding.

God is close to all.

God is not a hypothesis.

God is not moved by quantity but by quality.

† God loves you more than the devil hates you.

God metes out perfect justice
and perfect mercy.

God never judges men by their intellects,
but by their hearts.

God reasons with our requests.

God reveals His nature at
His own speed and time.

God seems cruel and indefinite
only to the selfish soul.

God speaks man's language.

God's favorites are those who obey Him.

*God's grace is
mankind's greatest thought.*

God's infinite power is
focused according to His will.

God's physical laws remain unwritten.

God's will cannot be
separated from His Word.

God's will is His way.

Have you felt God's presence
in the gentle breeze?

Hold fast to God;
you are living on a moving earth.

It is impossible to be truly great
without God's approval on your life.

Let God make music
on the strings of your heart.

Mankind does not define sin to God.

Many people feel justified in cheating God.

No one can see the time on God's clock.

Obedience to God is the only assurance
of living happily ever after.

*Obedience to God is
the only way to be good.*

On the first day God created the Light—
of knowledge about Himself.

Only God can bend the moon into a crescent.

Only God can express
the pity this sad world needs.

Only God can see the wounded soul.

Only God can understand
the atheism of the atheist.

Only God knows the depth
of your personality.

Peace with God is always on His terms.

Many people complain of God's willingness and
power to forgive another person's sins.

Since God had no beginning,
how could He have an ending?

Since we cannot understand ourselves,
how can we expect to understand God?

Suppose God dealt with you as you really are.

The armor that God gives is Himself.

The atheist doesn't know Who's good for him.

The Bible is mankind's insight
into God's mind.

The courses in the school
of God's education are tough.

The fire God ignites within
has its own peculiar glow.

The first light was God's voice.

The glory of God is
the summation of all that He is.

The wealth of God's grace is
not distributed denominationally.

There is a big difference between
our God and our god.

There will come a time when
all you have is God.

To be great in God's eyes is all that matters.

*What is life's purpose
if not serving God?*

What is your name for God?

When God visits, be sure you're at home.

When we are standing with God,
all else appears small.

"Whosoever" expresses
the depth of God's love.

*Within every person is
a hunger for God.*

Your blessings don't come from
what God does, but from Him.

Good/Bad;
Right/Wrong

A fool is never right on purpose.

A good man obeys because it is right.

A good start is no excuse for a bad ending.

A good thought is a valuable treasure.

A hunger for good indicates a healthy appetite.

A law never made a bad man good.

A man's will may argue against the right,
but he usually knows what to do.

A perversion is always wrong.

A rogue is suspicious of a good man.

A small mind thinks
all is wrong that is above it.

Abiding in Jesus is right personified.

Being right is sometimes an inconvenience.

Being right with God
brings mankind and its needs very near.

Can you call it pain if it is good for you?

Crave good choices.

Creating the opportunity to do good
is to be great.

Doing good is better than planning well.

Doing good is not enough—we must do right.

Don't attempt to bring good down
to a convenient level.

Every talent, whether it be used for
good or ill, came from a loving God.

Evil has more martyrs than does good.

Forming a good habit takes effort;
bad habits come unbidden.

Good advice comes forthrightly.

Good makes allowance for evil.
Evil never returns the favor.

Good will is not expressed in many words.

Goodness is a personal decision.

Hating evil is not enough.
You must fill its place with good.

Have you felt the cold,
clammy presence of evil?

If a child wants to do it,
is it necessarily wrong?

If you are right, you need no defense.

*Ignorance has few answers
and they are usually wrong.*

In every organization,
strong persons are needed
who will stand for the right.

In philosophy, the concepts of good
and true cannot be excelled.

Intolerance in the face of evil is just.

Is it hypocrisy to appear bad
when you are good?

It doesn't matter if you miss the wrong road.

It is good to perceive that we are pursued,
if not by truth then certainly by evil.

It is often a more emotional experience
to be proven right than to be found wrong.

*Keep an honest comparison between
good and evil.*

Laws do not persuade a person to do right.

Liberty is the freedom to do right.

Mankind's greatest ability is
that of choosing right or wrong.

Misers misspell good, making it gold.

Morals make you good, not dreary.

Neither pleasure nor pain is the chief good.

Obedience to God is the only way to be good.

Oh, the sheer pleasure of not saying
the right thing at the wrong time!

Opposition has difficulty when you are right.

Right comes by faith
and obedience to God's Word.

Right has its consequences.

Right or wrong is
never decided on the battlefield.

*Right reason comes from
sound knowledge.*

Some folks are on the right road
but are going the wrong way.

Some people are as happy when they do
wrong as others are when they do right.

The angriest person is the one who knows
he's wrong and won't admit it.

The gambler pays to have bad luck.

The good life is always uphill.

The means to grasp a right idea
is to act upon it.

The one who is right
seldom offers a compromise.

The only right thing to do again is right.

The only way to be good is to do good.

The persecuted side is usually the right one.

The pleasure of wrong shows its power.

The right path often starts with adversity.

The satisfaction of being right should not be
proving another person wrong.

The spirit of rebellion is wrong.

The whole town should feel
the influence of a good man.

The world cannot shame a virtuous person.

*There is a difference between
feeling right and being right.*

There is a trinity of evil thoughts:
those toward yourself, those toward others,
and those toward God.

To hunger after good
gives one a healthy appetite.

Too often, the wrong way
seems to be the most reasonable.

Vice is more contagious than virtue.

Where one has suffered for good,
there is holy ground.

Why attack the motive
when the product is good?

Wrong assumptions cloud reason.

Wrong is the perversion of right.

You don't have to be wrong to be different.

You hold the ultimate freedom—
that of choosing right or wrong.

Your good qualities help others.

GREATNESS

A great man does not ask
for shallow experiences.

A person of greatness
doesn't use it to his own advantage.

Don't measure your importance
by public opinion.

Ease and greatness are incompatible.

*Graciousness is shown
in great people.*

Great men may have great faults.

Great minds are fulfilled in doing good.

Great people do great things.

*Great people help others
to live more fruitful lives.*

Great souls suffer in silence.

Greatness comes not by accident.

Greatness is not in the design.

It is impossible to be great
without adherence to biblical principles.

It is the plodder, and not the aggressor,
who accomplishes great things.

It may take many good men
to produce one great man.

Material assets do not prove greatness.

Most great persons stand alone.

No one is great without being responsible.

One rises to greatness; he never falls into it.

*Only great people know
the glory of being good.*

People who call themselves great
may seek to destroy good.

Some men cast a light
while others cast a shadow.

Strive to love those who are great.

*The great man's secret is
his loyalty to truth.*

The greatest man is
one who chooses right without reserve.

The greatest soldier is he who promotes life.

The influence of a great person never dies.

The server in the church is
greater than the ruler.

The truly great person
seldom notices his honest competition.

Why are so many people in our time
seemingly great but not good?

You are great if you can
undo acts wrongly done.

You may be great without being famous.

*Young man, be great,
not by what you do
but by what you are.*

HAPPINESS

A man is happy according to his wisdom.

A pleasant memory is no accident.

Are you ready to pray, "Lord,
make me happy according to my holiness"?

Be happy that life's dregs settle.

Be sure your laughter shows
the goodness of your heart.

Before wishing "Happy New Year," consider,
"What is happy?"

Character reveals itself by its laughter.

Don't flaunt your happiness.

Don't look for happiness; it's a by-product.

Few idle people are happy.

Happiness and action are cousins.

Happiness consists somewhat of
the ability to look straight ahead.

Happiness is a convenience, not a necessity.

Happiness is a seldom-traveled path.

Happiness is not assured by love alone.

*Happiness is work
that satisfies the soul.*

Happiness usually expands
when it is shared with others.

Happy is he who doesn't need
to beg his happiness from others.

He who expects to be happy generally is.

Holy people will be happy.

How long would the day be if
you counted only the happy hours?

I didn't know I was sad until I became happy.

If happiness is your goal,
prepare for a rough ride.

In order to be happy, be faithful.

It is better to err on the side of happiness.

It is extremely difficult to
keep happiness to one's self.

It is possible to be loved and still be unhappy.

It is wrong to lavish happiness on yourself.

It takes little effort to keep
a happy person happy.

Jesus' first miracle was to
expand His friends' happiness.

Jesus offered happiness only with conditions.

Laughter can conquer worry.

Neither wealth nor poverty assures happiness.

No busy person is entirely sad.

No one is happy by accident.

Pity those who laugh without smiling.

Pondering happiness may bring sadness.

Pray that your wisdom precedes your happiness.

The happy person usually loves truth.

The nearer wants and needs correspond,
the greater the happiness.

*The sad person may be
made more so when
remembering happy moments.*

The secular man's happiness is
often dependent upon his illusions.

To analyze happiness is to invite sadness.

To be happy, be interesting.

To be happy is the best cosmetic.

To be happy is to
supply intellectual light but not heat.

To be happy, you must be cheerful.

To some, being happy means being less sad.

Too many people think that a thumb
on the scales of life will bring happiness.

Unhappiness dislikes the contented.

Unhappy persons are usually
uninterested or uninteresting.

Virtue alone is the source of happiness.

We are as happy as we are helpful.

Wealth can be a curse if it is not a source of
happiness.

Woe to the society where the fool appears
happier than the saint.

*Your laugh reaches my ears,
but your smile reaches my heart.*

Honesty

A leader who is not straightforward in his integrity does not deserve the title.

A selfish spirit promotes dishonesty.

Adversity helps determine honesty.

Being accused by an honest man is different from being accused by a rogue.

Few people can deal honestly with reality.

Honest people are often lonely.

Hope enlarges courage.

Hope should not be dimmed by pleasure.

If you want to be one in a thousand,
be honest.

If you wish to astonish your enemies,
live with simple integrity.

*Integrity needs no cloak of
secrecy and mystery.*

Integrity will never deceive you.

It is easier to be honest with others
than with yourself.

Lying is not a talent.

Nothing destroys a friendship
quicker than untruth.

The evil person is never truly happy.

The honest man thinks true.

The irate man is usually honest about himself.

There is a severe battleground
between hope and despair.

To be honest is to be consistent.

To be trusted is better than to be loved.

Virtue stands on discipline.

Your honesty should never be a disadvantage.

HOPE

Frustration may be the kindling needed to
ignite a roaring fire of hope.

Hope and curiosity are close relatives.

Hope and disappointment are
often tethered together.

Hope and fear keep love alive.

Hope is an effective medicine.

Hope is the only medicine some can afford.

Hope keeps the heart from breaking.

Hope looks for the reasonable path.

Hope should increase with the years.

Human hope is the most deceitful.

Keep looking at the light
and you will not see the darkness.

Psychiatry lives life in the past;
steadfast hope drives it forward.

The Bible is not a book of despair.

The gospel fulfills every hope.

There's hope in patience.

Those who look for the worst
in any situation usually find it.

True hope is not
expecting something for nothing.

JESUS

All that is good is because of Jesus.

Jesus came into your life to live
and to make you alive.

Jesus can enter only the open heart.

Jesus did not say, "You will build my church."

Jesus gave no example for killing.

Jesus is mankind's highest authority.

Jesus is still the Master Teacher.

Jesus is the truth that sets us free.

Jesus practiced what He preached.

Jesus reveals Himself to those who obey Him.

News headlines proclaim: World Needs Jesus.

Only Jesus' burden is light.

Some people hear temptation's tap
but cannot hear Jesus' knock.

The divine Trinity did not condense into
Jesus, but was magnified in Him.

There is no higher learning
other than knowing Jesus.

Try to say Jesus without smiling.

You can't clean up this world with soap;
it takes Jesus' blood.

JUDGING

Actions are being misjudged
more often than words.

Don't judge greatness by your own standard.

Don't judge your hunger by others' appetites.

*Injustice is bearable;
justice is tough.*

Justice will never arise out of injustice.

Never judge an organization
by those who leave it.

Never question your judgment
when dealing with a rascal.

One way to handle a chronic liar is
to listen while his lies judge him.

Only God can judge whether
a task is great or small.

Strong judgment rests in a lively imagination.

The stone you throw may hit you.

Thinking long is usually thinking right.

Which do you most desire, mercy or justice?

Which do you most give to others,
mercy or justice?

KINDNESS

A broken heart needs
the soothing music of a kind word.

Being right does not rule out being kind.

Doing good starts small.

If you can't be nice, be kind.

Kindness is a self-multiplier.

Kindness is based on morality.

Kindness is one of life's treasured sentiments.

Kindness would be more effective
if it started at home.

Make a list of kind words and use them often.

The source of praise is usually a kind heart.

Too many people are kind
for their own advantage.

Who is most apt to be kind,
a man or a woman?

Why are groups more often cruel
while the individuals in them may be kind?

LOVE

Am I a faithful sample of
Jesus' love to the world?

A person who knows not how to love, knows
not how to worship.

A wound made by a lover is slow to heal.

As my solitude expanded,
my love for God deepened.

Be someone whom children love.

Be worthy of love.

Beware of the people who make their living
from those they say they love.

Can the world tell by your lifestyle
that you love?

Can you love someone you do not trust?

Everyone needs a child's love.

Every thing a man loves
he believes is beautiful.

Flowers are God's love picture.

Good things happen when
we love our superiors.

*Harmony is warm words
wrapped in love.*

He who loves the most
experiences the greater suffering.

Heed the advice of those who love you.

If beauty is in the eye of the beholder,
beauty is the invitation to love.

If someone tramples you,
protect him with your love.

It is difficult to define the attraction
of our love.

It is difficult to keep secrets
from those we love and trust.

It is great to keep falling in love anew
with the same woman, your wife.

It is impossible for love to remain static.

Let your heart be a healing hospital
for wounded souls.

Love and concern are the antidote for hatred.

Love can be lost.

*Love cannot be bought;
it can only be given.*

Love does not need an unlocked door.

Love doesn't need to shout.

Love, even though your heart
is sometimes small.

Love faithfully.

Love goodness.

Love illuminates.

Love is a twined thread.

Love is not self-sustaining.

Love is the easiest emotion to counterfeit.

Love is the harvest of kindness.

Love is the only antidote for anger.

Love knows the greatest pain.

Love makes it possible to think young.

Love never proves—it confesses.

Love never reacts; it responds.

Love proves "God is Love."

Love reaches out.

Love spurned creates a bruise.

Love the child.

Love them because they are your children.

Love turns warmer at evening time.

Love wants to be held to be kept warm.

Lovers are natural helpers.

Loving only those who love us
takes variety out of life.

Lust is unaffected by love.

Many children don't know a parent's love
until they are parents.

Never edit a love letter.

O, the security of a lover's love!

Revere the tears of a mother.

Spurned love is costly.

The beauty of love is to love
without understanding its object.

The essence of love is self-sacrifice.

The ink in a lover's pen runs warm.

The lover is generous.

The lover's soul never grows old.

They are not in love, just in like.

To enlarge your soul, love a child.

To flatter is not to love.

To love is to desire.

To vow to love is to anticipate sorrow.

True charity expects no rewards.

Unrenewed love exhausts itself.

We can trust those who love much.

We forgive only to the extent we love.

We love because we esteem.
We esteem because we love.

We never forget those we love.

We often love others for the good
they have allowed us to do for them.

When a person speaks of love,
it is usually an autobiography.

When you are loved,
the impossible becomes probable.

When you smile, make it a smile of love.

Whisper when speaking of love.

With all my faults, I love you anyway.

You can best witness God's love to others
when your heart is broken.

*Your love of God is
your only proof of love.*

MISCELLANEOUS
CHILDREN

A child and a genius
have one thing in common: curiosity.

A child's cry hurts the same in any language.

*A child's grief and a man's sorrow
may weigh the same.*

Are adults ever produced outside of
the influence of children?

Children are most often punished for
their parents' mistakes.

It is much better to be childlike
than to be childish.

Seldom force a child to be idle.
The secret is to focus energy.

You are old when you are
no longer Mama's child.

*Your children should be treated as
guests in your home.*

FAILURE

Doing what you please may bring
total failure or great success.

If you have never failed in anything,
you are missing a valuable experience.

It is not necessary for others to fail
in order for one to succeed.

Many people enter a new enterprise
with a spirit of failure.

Our failures teach us life's values.

Some people work hard to fail
while others just fail.

To stumble doesn't mean to fall.

Trying and failing usually gives
opportunity to try again.

We learn most from our failures.

JOY

A tear may be a telescope
focusing on heaven's joys.

Joy and sorrow are cousins.

Joy can be shared; pain, never.

Joy comes to him who scatters joy.

Joy demands companionship.

Should a man's cries of pain be louder
than his shouts of joy?

PEACE

No one can measure the peace of silence.
Peace comes quietly in the heart.

Peace is in God's will.

Peace is more difficult to understand than war.

Peace is the fruit of righteousness.

Personal peace is greater than joy.

The way to find peace outside
is to have it inside.

THANKSGIVING

A conservative knows and appreciates
not only the present but also the past.

Be grateful you don't have all the answers.

Deep gratitude speaks in low tones.

Don't just be thankful; be grateful.

Gratitude is a noble passion.

Gratitude is in the heart of one who has accomplished a long night.

Happiness is linked with gratitude.

Thanksgiving is the right reason for giving.

MONEY

A billionaire can't count his money.

*A miser is one who
lives poor to die rich.*

A miser is one who seems to be
unhappy about money.

If you think money is not a blessing,
try to contribute something you don't have.

It is easier to conceal poverty than riches.

It is right to have money,
but don't desire more than another person.

It's not what you possess that makes you rich,
but what you have given away.

Judas sold himself for thirty pieces of silver.

Money cannot speak to the wise person.

Money helped the Good Samaritan
achieve his title.

Money in itself is worthless;
its only value is in what it can purchase.

Money increases in value
when it is shared with others.

Much of life for some people is
trying to get someone else's money.

Of what value is money but to use it.

One may live rich without being wealthy.

Riches do not make the wise man unhappy.

Sometimes rich people feel poor because
they lack all their desires.

The destitute don't bear the
weighty problems of wealth.

The one who plays the lottery pays to lose.

The rich man is jealous of what he has;
the poor man is jealous of what he has not.

*The richest man shows
no material wealth.*

The search for money and the search for truth
are usually in different locations.

Those who demand life's paycheck
are perpetually poor.

Thrift is a golden harvest.

To be rich is to find wealth
and then give it to another.

Too many people it seems work hard
to be the richest in the cemetery.

We are warned of germs on money,
but who was ever sick of money?

Wealth awakens selfishness.

Wealth has two forms: living and dead.

MUSIC

A rest in music beautifies it.
The same is true in life.

Good music gives us the
happy homesick feeling for places
we've never been.

Good music is Satan's enemy.

How many beautiful songs float,
unwritten, in the air?

*Music can aid and
enliven every passion.*

Music shouted; the baby cried.
Music whispered; the man wept.

O, let music guide me to heaven's gate.

*The best way to carry music
is in your heart.*

The melody of music is in your heart,
never on paper.

The order of a person's music advertises the
state of his mind.

The same musical score can both break
and mend the heart.

To some people, music is agreeable noise;
to others, it is the essence of the soul.

Was music better when it was young?

Woe be to him who first perverted
the sweetness of music.

POTPOURRI

A candle is enlightening company.

A chip on the shoulder may
create a knot on the head.

A clear mind has many adversaries.

A committee is often
a cemetery of good ideas.

A complete autobiography is impossible.

A deceiver is easily deceived.

A deep thought is always a clear one.

A doubter may merely be a deep thinker.

A face-to-face meeting often erases bitterness.

A fool will learn only by
experience and sometimes not then.

*A good exercise for the heart is
to bend down and help another up.*

A good loser should expect to lose.

A great person
foregoes personal advantage over others.

A hard person overlooks virtue
to focus on weaknesses.

A heavy heart can break of its own weight.

A leader must by definition act alone.

A learned fool is the larger one.

A lingering farewell is painful to the soul.

A loving wife is a husband's magnetic pole.

A pleasant memory is no accident.

A positive thinker is more believable.

A thinker thrives in
the rough current that pushes against him.

A weed is a plant in the wrong place.

Actions do not need a tongue to speak.

Adam must have forgotten
to have dominion over himself.

All of nature is a silent gospel.

An emotional bruise takes a long time to heal.

Are others benefiting from your knowledge?

Birds are known by their chirp; people are, too.

Blowing doesn't make a flutist.

Boldness is not arrogance.

Boredom leads to cruelty.

Brevity may be obscurity.

Brushing doesn't make a painter.

Burning your life's candle at both ends
gives a brilliant but brief light.

Buzzards don't learn much from wrens.

Bystanders become cruel when
watching violence.

Can a good husband be less than a genius?

Can a man have a small mind
but a large heart?

Can I have your heart
merely by giving you mine?

Can we give a gift
that costs us nothing?

Can you shine without burning yourself away?

Candlelight softens the emotions.

Chaos has a sound all its own.

Character is formed by
knowledge, heat, and pressure.

Character reveals moral purpose.

*Charity is more than
giving the poor good advice.*

Charm is to make another person comfortable.

Check your weaknesses when
prompted to advise others.

Cherish reason much more than
you cherish feelings.

Choose choices well.

Circumstances are short; ability lasts a lifetime.

Commitment always requires surrender.

Committees often complicate simplicity.

Common sense keeps life from
becoming too difficult.

Confidence is reciprocal.

Consecrate your intellect to God;
in turn, He will expand it.

Could you plead guilty of
being a good person?

Cruelty is weakness.

Danger thrives on both fear and confidence.

Darkness cannot extinguish light.

Dear Lord, let me die with light
and not with darkness.

Deep, loving emotions can be
shared without a sound.

Define the five loaves and two fish
you give to God.

Denying God's existence
does not void His laws.

Desires are necessary to keep life moving.

Despair completes loneliness.

Determination is better than strength.

Determine the impossibility of a situation by
the number of suggestions offered.

Did God give lightning for the sighted
and thunder for the blind?

Did I make the world around me better today?

Did the atheist create himself?

Did you know that everyone is lonely?

Difficulty is an effective instructor.

Difficulty promotes excellence.

Directly or indirectly,
your influence affects the whole world.

Discernment is a cultivated gift.

Discontent promotes progress.

Disobedience is rebellion in action.

Do you care that apathy is
society's greatest problem?

Don't advertise yourself like a skunk.

Don't expect a crooked man to walk straight.

Don't make a pet out of your peeve.

*Education too often takes
the form of ritual.*

Emotions are trainable.

*Encouragement accomplishes more
than correction.*

Enthusiasm is found in
the soul of every genius.

Enthusiasm promotes the same in others.

Envy and jealousy bring no profit.

Equals need no protocol.

Even the greatest books were written
one word at a time.

Even while speaking,
some folks have nothing to say.

Every fence has two sides.

Every leader must be controversial
in order to be effective.

Every man has his own ethic
by which he will live or die.

Every person longs for sincerity and certainty.

Everyone, living or dead,
has an eternal destiny.

Everyone needs a personal cathedral.

Everything we do affects others.

Everything we receive from God is a gift.

Excess doubt tears the soul.

Excuses may be confessions.

Executing a good idea is
the only way to keep it from dying.

Experience is the past tense of circumstances.

Experience is to be shared.

Experiences, more than education, build a
great life.

Facts won't argue with your theories.

False charity soon runs aground.

Farewell is a word that is seldom shouted.
Fate grovels in the dirt.

Favor arrives discreetly.

Fetters are always painful,
regardless of their material.

Few people can deal honestly with reality.

Fiery trials may produce heavenly light.

*Fill your basket with fruit and
you will have no room for trash.*

Foolish actions are harder to
confess than wrong ones.

Give each person you meet today
something pleasant to remember you by.

Give me your testimony, not your argument.

Giving God your sins is not a sacrifice,
but giving Him yourself is.

God has given you a job to do;
do you appreciate the honor?

God may use our injuries to bless others.

Good advice contains few words.

Good advice never costs anybody anything.

Good is not a reaction to evil.

Gossips don't revere a gossip.

Greed feeds on gain and pride.
Greed increases with the growing hoard.

Growth must deal with controversy.

Habits multiply in kind.

Hammering doesn't make a carpenter.

Hatred is a form of self-punishment.

Hatred is a hard pillow.

Hatred is a low estate,
but it reaches to the highest levels of society.

Have a higher life's ambition than to grow old.

Have you ever known an enthusiastic cynic?

Having all the pieces is
no guarantee the puzzle can be assembled.

Having no alternative is
the best strategy for leadership.

He couldn't see a hole in a sieve.

He doesn't hold a grudge; he throws it at you.

*He is the true leader
who touches the heart.*

He may say nothing but speak volumes.

He needed no flame to make his blood boil.

He seemed to live life in a minor key.

He should have a great education
if he learns by his mistakes.

He who confesses easily confesses often.

He who discourages you is your master.

Hypocrites may be found in any organization.

I deserve my character.

I should know the Shepherd better than
His Twenty-Third Psalm.

Idleness tempts the devil.

If I wait to do greater things
until I do the lesser, why do anything?

If only old age had strength
and youth had knowledge.

If the world is a book,
study the sidebars and footnotes.

If the world is cold, warm it with your heart.

If you are accomplishing a difficult task,
do your own grunting.

If you are false to God,
you will never be true to another.

If you are satisfied with a little,
what would you do with a lot?

*If you ask a question,
you must be prepared for the answer.*

If you don't learn by your mistakes,
why bother making them?

If you find a path with no obstacles,
it probably doesn't lead anywhere.

If you had more, where would you put it?

*If you have a loving heart
you will speak loving words.*

If you think life is brief,
you haven't been in a dentist's chair.

If you want to be pitied, complain.

If your hearers laugh,
you know they are hearing you.

Ignorance and pride are close relatives.

Ignorance is a long night.

Illusion: Not knowing
whether your eyes are open or closed.

Imagination and custom are usually at odds.
Imagination spurs enthusiasm.

In a crisis, everything is important.

In God's plan, spirit, soul, and body
are kept in harmony.

In human experience, it takes less to
build a wall than to build a bridge.

Indiscretion has no benefits.

*It is better to deal with a problem
than to cope with it.*

It is possible for a person to stand tall
and still be humble.

Keep a loose grip on your possessions
so if they leave, you don't.

Keep your anchor rope as short as possible.

*Knowledge has a price
that few are willing to pay.*

Labels do not cover nakedness.

Lawyers would make a difficult living if
people kept their promises.

Leaders lead naturally.

Learn about a person by the way that
he describes another person's character.

Learn to say hard things in a soft way.

Learning by other's mistakes is much less costly.

Learning is a series of discoveries.
Lessons taught by pain are seldom forgotten.

Let each day be a beginning.

Let me see the rising sun;
the sunset is too sad.

Let my tottering be only forward.

Let the light of your counsel
have warmth, too.

*Let your desires be limited
only by the Holy Spirit.*

Let's see evolution build a house.

Liars are cowards.

Liberty allows society's cream to rise.

Life is a multitude of ordinary days.

Life is both slippery and rough.

Life is the lengthy training to be old.

Life is what happens.

*Life's answers are seldom
in response to the questions asked.*

Light's reflection on water
reveals nothing of the deep.

Like the bee, you can't make honey
and sting at the same time.

Listen for the meaning in
what you have to say.

*Live so that your example will be
a positive precedent.*

Live that the world considers you a necessity.

Live that when you die, your ideas don't.

Make sure your heart is
more attractive than your face.

Make yourself necessary.

Man cannot determine the size
of his good intentions.

Maturity is not measured by
accumulated years.

Meat always has bones.

No matter what the body posture,
keep your soul on its knees.

No one appreciates an unthankful person.

No one arrives in heaven by accident.

*No one arrives
in heaven unexpectedly.*

No one can measure the strength of
his imagination.

No one repents of tenderness.

No one reveres a malcontent.

No one understands despair.

Not all growth is an increase.

Nothing is done while planning.

Nothing raises productivity like respect.

Nothing symbolizes
man's restless heart like the sea.

Nursing homes seem to be
God's waiting rooms.

O, the great difference between
strength and perseverance.

*Often the simplest ideas come from
the most complex minds.*

Old age should whiten not only the hair but
also the soul.

On every battlefield,
the spirit of Cain comes to life again.

*One hears best when
he listens with his heart.*

One who cheats others will
undoubtedly cheat himself.

One who is a slave of his opinions is a cripple.

Only a fool presumes on God's grace.

Only a fool will argue with a fool.

Only God can express the pity
this sad world needs.

Only the Carpenter of Nazareth
can repair our broken world.

Only you are qualified to
bear your responsibilities.

Other people's sins
do not make you righteous.

Others' strengths can
minister to my weakness.

Our compassion for the people
of the world should grow as
our knowledge of them expands.

Our duty is not to see through one another,
but to see one another through.

Our life ethic is
often based on custom.

Pain: the great mystery.

Patient attention is the root of any discovery.

People can tell an artificial sweetener.

People long for sincerity and certainty.

Personal feelings may be personal foolings.

Philosophy deals with the head and ignores the heart.

Pillows seem to aid answers to
difficult questions.

Pity the genius who knows much about little.

Pity the leader who must prove himself.

Pleasant memories are a soft cushion
for the bruises of old age.

Pleasing God is freedom.

Poverty stirs generosity.

Power has no need to speak of itself.

Power is a false gratification.

Practical knowledge is usually self-acquired.

Pray for the marriage of ability and ambition.

Prejudice is a thriving emotion.

Preserve in your heart even the small comforts
in order to pass them on to others.

Presumption destroys more than despair.

Problems come to all people,
but some folks barely take time to notice.

Prophecies are often disguised as jest.

Quiet reserve exalts the heart.

Quiet virtues are best.

Raising your voice is a poor way to
reinforce your argument.

Rare is he who cannot say
one thing and mean another.

Rashness is firmness gone to seed.

Reaching heaven is the supreme graduation.

Reason and reasons may be strangers.

Red roses have a language of their own.

Repentance borders on innocence.

Repose is not laziness.

Respect the opinions of those who
have come through distress victoriously.

Rights always require responsibility.

Sadness is the shadow of something larger.

Scars always follow falsehoods.

*Scatter sweet words and
soft thoughts as you go.*

Seasonings may destroy the original flavor.

Second thoughts are most deceiving.

Seldom does an open heart have closed lips.

Self-discipline and free expression
promote service to others.

Self-esteem is not the same as self-importance.

Sense tomorrow's weaknesses today.

Sentiments are inherited through traditions.

Show me a man who uses his own backbone.

Sign your name with loving deeds.

Silence expresses the inexpressible.

Silence is a dangerous excuse for inaction.

Silence is more awesome than noise.

Silence may be a lie.

Silence may be the best way to
express some thoughts.

Simple favors are best.

Simple words sound better.

Sin can be contagious.

Sincerity and generosity make a delightful pair.

Sincerity does not prove value.

Sincerity is no shield against stupidity.

Sincerity requires strength.

Skill is controlled by tact.

Slander is a two-edged sword.

Slavery weakens society's character.

Society happens when two lives join.

Society's strongest law is custom.

Society's worst habit is indecision.

Solitude is an interesting companion.

Solitude permits one to walk
the hallways of his mind
to peer into rooms of forgotten memories.

Some curse their bad habits but cling to them.

Some folks accomplish more by
accident than others do on purpose.

Some folks are greatly entertained
through your listening to them talk.

Some folks can see only what
needs to be done.

Some folks seem always to be
beginning to begin.

Sometimes education is unlearning.

*Strength grows in
the presence of opposition.*

Suppose God would actually give you the
tough time you think you are now having.

Take it easy, Dad; it's difficult being young.

Talent is unselfish.

Talents are disclosed in tragedy.

Tenderness arises at night.

Thankless jobs are often the most essential.

The advice of the afflicted is easy to ignore.

The aggressor may be a victim of
his own brutality.

The agnostic simply doesn't know.

The art of deceiving
involves the craft of pleasing.

The bigger the heart,
the more quickly broken.

The boldness to reprove should equal
the sinner's daring to sin.

The braggart is the ultimate idealist.

The bridle is to guide, not to restrict.

The chain's weakest link controls the rest.

The changing shadow of sunshine on the wall
proves the earth is moving.

The clenched fist is not a sign of strength
but the open hand reaching out to help is.

The compassionate person has
great influence on other people.

The covetous person wants
but never possesses.

*The Cross cannot be a symbol;
it is a stark reality.*

The crowd was the only beast in the arena.

The cure for your birth
is to live right.

The cynic and the optimist both think
they are observing reality.

The cynic is an emotional weakling.

The daily paper should not be
a vessel of contained vanities.

The devil has his martyrs, too.

The disappointed pessimist is really sad.

The discontented mind
cannot reason sweet thoughts.

The divine Trinity is not a committee.

The easy life leads to atheism.

The egotist uses any means,
usually despicable, to advance his goals.

The emotions of the moment
return with the memory.

The envious are afraid of self-excellence.

The evolutionist and the atheist
cannot see man as a complete person.

The eyes speak many languages.

The face is often the title page to
the volume of the life.

The faint of heart needs a shoulder to lean on.
Give him one of yours.

The falling leaf is more symbolic
of life than a springing bud.

The firefly glows when it is ascending.

The flesh is never satisfied because
it is alive and it gets hungry.

The fool craves impossibilities.

The form grief takes is usually a memory.

The fortunate are they who can
bear misfortune.

The fragrance of His presence
pervaded each of those in the room,
uniting them in sweet fellowship.

The freedom to live above the law is the right
to drive under the speed limit.

The giants among you are those who
refused to allow others to
whittle them down to a smaller size.

The greatest deeds are done
in a fragment of time.

*The greatest question:
What will you do?*

The greatest rebuke to the world and the devil
is a life of quiet obedience to God.

The handwriting on the wall
still terrifies most people.

The hardest secret to keep is one of your own.

The heretic is much more dangerous
than the sinner.

The humanist futilely looks for
natural causes in supernatural events.

*The ideal is light that enlightens
and warmth that comforts.*

The incarnation proves the masculinity of God.

The indecisive person has a pillow of thorns.

The indecisive person has lost his moral code.

The indecisive person is self-destructive.

The innocent person doesn't need to explain.

The insincere cannot recognize the sincere.

The integrity of every man is
measured by his conduct.

The jealous person is the most insecure.

The jealous person punishes
himself with his own methods.

The lack of wit may be
more ridiculous than its excess.

The liar usually has difficulty
believing anyone else.

The life's motivation of many is
their own stubbornness.

The lightning is God's autograph.

The little you give
may be great to the recipient.

The loneliest person is one who
is hiding from himself.

The person who knows little, suspects much.

The same wind that extinguishes the candle
increases the forest fire.

The thorns and the blossom are
equal parts of the rose.

The weaker argument asks for a compromise.

To wonder is the basis of life.

Too much risk is better than excess precaution.

Too often,
circumstance is blamed for human delay.

Too often in religious matters,
solid values sink and trifles arise to the fore.

Too often, one's lamp goes out while
he decides in which direction to go.

Too often, the aggressor pleads he is
merely defending himself.

Too often, the exchange of gifts becomes
a system of trading.

Too often, the last voice victory hears is,
"It can't be done."

Twilight softens the emotions.

Unrest of soul gives impetus to life.

Valleys need mountains to touch the sky.

Valor holds its greatness in any circumstance.

Valor is composed of doing your duty.

Variety is a source of pleasure.

Vices require a small diet to thrive.

Virtue entails self-sacrifice.

Virtue is a wonderful habit.

Virtue is life's perfume.

Virtue is not always restraint;
it is usually the right uses of opportunity.

Wanting is a greater power than having.

Wants define the man.

We all have deeps and shallows.

We are indebted to our benefactors.

We are made by our decisions.

We are startled by our thoughts' depth.

We cannot see our true selves,
even in a mirror.

We cannot tell by outward appearance
the aging of the soul.

We can't avoid error if
we don't know what it is.

We don't know the extent of our influence
over another person.

We learn to know people by our going
to them rather than by their coming to us.

We like people who say what we think.

We may anticipate tomorrow like a veteran,
but when it arrives,
we are once again life's novices.

We often form our opinions of people
by their abilities.

We seldom learn but are always learning.

We tend to act more with our desires
than our powers.

*We write our names on others' hearts
by our words and actions.*

Weakness promotes falsehood.

Wealth awakens selfishness.

What a person knows should be
expressed in what he does.

What color is solitude?

What color is your voice?

What did I give away today?

What do you call the space between
the optimist and the pessimist?

What folly it is to be in a prison
of your own making.

What have I done worthy of a compliment?

What we have been makes us what we are.

What would you pay to be a millionaire?

When a man stands alone,
he usually stands against culture.

When casting off public opinion,
be certain to rise above it.

When greeting someone, compliment them.

When I die, let me say, "It is finished."

When it comes to evangelism,
some folks stop at nothing.

When offering a hand to another,
give your whole self.

When one learns to die, it's over.

*When one serves his family,
he also graces society.*

When reason and habit argue, the talk is brief.

When speaking to a group, talk to individuals.

When you are in pain,
lose yourself in gentle thoughts.

When you die, your hands will open.

When you look in the mirror,
you should see an important person.

When you rebuke, don't be contentious.

Where are laws in wartime?

Where does moderation stand
while facing extremes?

Where is solitude when the crowds appear?

Where would you be if Adam
had not been lonely?

Which do you value most:
your rights or your privileges?

Who can explain a rose?

Who else can an egotist talk about?

Who is responsible when a ball game is
more exciting than a sermon?

Who ministers to the minister?

Who will be your leaning staff when
you are old and infirm?

Why do I take personal attacks personally?

Why do some people use guns
in a spiritual battle?

Why do we countenance the opinions
of those who dislike us?

Why promise when you can do?

Wickedness is a cancer.

Will the crowds always call to save Barabbas?

With age we become more like ourselves.

*Words are the most fragile mode
of communication.*

Words break hearts, not bones.

Worry if your weak points are applauded.

Would you rather have strength or power?

Would you rather light your life's candle,
or let a mouse eat it?

Would you speak up if your life was
about to be aborted?

Wouldn't it be great if people naturally
grew better with age?

You don't have to look at the clock to know
that time is running out.

You give lasting impressions
to everyone you meet.

You must be a force before you can be resisted.

*Your character is
what you are all of the time.*

PRAISE

Enrich someone's life today
with a warm word of praise.

*God praises not success
but faithfulness.*

He who lives without praise is miserable.

How quick the world praises
the appearance of merit.

If men praise you,
it could be that you are like them.

In order to be just,
learn to praise only the finest things.

It is a habit to feel aloof from those we praise.

Many praise Jesus while giving
no thought to following Him.

*Never be the last to
praise a good work.*

No one praises personal jealousy.

Note whether he who
praises you deserves praise.

Praise genuinely.

Praise may lead to temptation.

Some people will interrupt
your praising them with helpful additions.

The humanist praises man for what is right
and blames God for what is wrong.

The jealous person attacks
what is praiseworthy in another person.

*The source of praise is
usually a kind heart.*

To praise is to participate in other's joy.

When a man hears praise,
he expects it to be a
just estimation of his qualities.

When a person praises you,
you may be on his path and not your own.

Prayer and Prayers

A prayer is not a wish that
we hope will come true.

*Are your words in silent and
verbal prayers the same?*

Dear God, here I stand
lifting my heart and my hands to You.

Dear God, please don't rush tomorrow
upon me. I haven't fully digested
the joys and sorrows of today.

Dear God, please let the
Light of the World illumine my way home;
I'm so afraid of the dark.

Dear God, the bumps and bruises
of today have been so difficult.
Should I look forward to tomorrow?

Dear God, when it comes my time to die,
please grant me the assurance that
Your loving arms are my cradle.

Dear heavenly Father, when my time comes to
die, let me not be envious of the living.

Dear Jesus,
I thank You especially for normal days.

Dear Jesus, this world has hurt me,
and I'm running home to You.

Dear Lord,
could I do entirely good just one day?

Dear Lord, help me.
I fell down and scratched my soul today.

Dear Lord, yesterday was such a happy day;
could I live it again, please?

Don't pray so loud; God is near.

Don't say "Amen" if you didn't hear the prayer.

Events that drive you to pray
can keep you from praying.

God doesn't need an answering machine.

I pray that at the end of life I will drop into
God's waiting hand as a piece of ripened fruit.

If my life is a written book,
dear God, please be my editor.

It doesn't take a long prayer
to get God's attention.

Make all your wishes worthy of a prayer to
your heavenly Father.

Most people live as they pray.

Never criticize God's answers to your prayers.

People who pray only when in trouble
must enjoy the trouble.

Please let me die with a smile on my face.

Pray that your life's book will
be better than its cover.

Praying is no substitute for obedience.

Silent prayers may reach heaven first.

The most desperate prayers are said when
you are on your back
rather than on your knees.

The sincere wish contains its own prayer.

There is no greater gift than a prayer to God for you.

When we talk on God's prayer line,
we never need to say "good-bye."

Your actions after praying are
more important than the prayer.

Your best prayer is not a request but praise.

READING AND WRITING

A writer knows the meaning of
the word "alone."

A writer may give birth
immediately upon conception.

A writer sees truth in the shiver of the wind,
the glow of the moon,
and the ache of the heart.

*A writer shapes words
into colorful patterns.*

A writer should be better than his work.

A writer who explains his work
is no longer a writer but a speaker.

A writer's true signature is his deepest thoughts.

Books and articles should be read
with the same objective as the authors'.

Creating astonishment at life is
the writer's greatest motive.

Don't merely be a good writer; write well.

Effective writing states
what others merely think.

*Every writer should
compose self-portraits.*

Good writing should resemble its author.

Great writers record good things
on others' hearts.

Humanity is the co-author of any manuscript.

Listen for an author's whispers.

Many read; few think.

Never read to avoid thinking.

One should always read to remember,
never to forget.

Read to find the author's meaning;
read again to find your own.

*Reading should produce
quotable thoughts.*

The problem isn't just writing,
but finding readers who comprehend.

The writer mixes brains with his ink.

The writer states more of what we think
than of what we say.

The writer writes; the reader interprets.

*When reading,
search for the author's intent.*

When writing,
promote only that worth remembering.

Write to be read, often.

Writing should simplify life, not obscure it.

Writing should tell the reader
how to enjoy life.

You cannot correct the writer's original proofs—
his character.

Self-Knowledge

A contented person is
generally looked upon with suspicion.

A selfish attitude is
the most difficult to confess.

A selfish spirit sums up all the sins of mankind.

Actions reveal thoughts.

Are you known for what you have
or for what you are?

Attempting to cover your faults
merely adds to them.

Be impatient with yourself, not with others.

Deal with your faults as carefully as
you would a painful splinter.

Don't laugh at the elderly;
you're looking at your future.

Emotionally stable persons grow
accustomed to attacks from unstable ones.

If spanking cures a child's carelessness,
would the same cure work for yours?

Knowledge is full of humor.

Many people lie when speaking of themselves.

No one brags about being a hypocrite.

Our cravings should not rule us.

Recognizing our faults does not excuse them.

Regret is not repentance.

Reputation speaks; character shouts!

Strong feelings do not prove a strong character.

The selfish person is unaware of true values.

The sincere person recognizes his faults in others and tries to correct himself.

There is plenty of pride in most humility.

You are a mixture of dust and deity.

Your uniqueness is God's gift to you.

SMILES

A smile is the preface to the man.

A smile will confuse your critics.

A warm smile is a good start toward filling
anyone's life with sweetness.

*Even an ugly person is
attractive when he smiles.*

Even when you are alone,
your smile should be self-enriching.

Make your smile more eye-catching than
a missing button.

One loving smile can erase
many doubting frowns.

Smiles are beautiful when tears are close.

Smiles are highly contagious.

The easiest farewell is a smile.

The greatest of personal influences is
a gentle smile.

The smile of understanding
gets a friendly one in return.

The way a person smiles reveals his character.

To live a life of victory,
cover an aching heart with a smile.

SPIRITUALITY

A holy life is the best theology.

A holy life means a life like Jesus'.

A joyful spirit is strong.

A man cannot make himself holy.

A man is hard pressed to live his religion.

A selfish spirit is always wrong.

Any peace that I have came from Jesus.

Avoid books in which honest meditation
is not enhanced.

Battling one's cross makes it heavier.

Be content; God chooses what is best for you.

Be sure that God's investment in you pays off.

Both a baby and a rock symbolize
Jesus' kingdom.

Can you sense your spiritual strength
in times of difficulty?

Can your religion pass the test of practicality?

Deep thoughts flow from
a broken, sincere heart.

Devotion to Jesus means
an abandonment of material values.

Emotional storms may flood the soul,
but a healthy spirit rises above it.

Every evening God pulls the drapes
on our busy day, allowing time for
reflection, confession, and rest.

Everyone who doesn't worship God
has his own idols.

Everything adds up to eternity.

Give God your troubles.
He will keep them forever,
or until you want them back again.

God doesn't make us
more godly than we want to be.

Godliness declines as religious forms increase.

Grace is clothing for the soul
as dress is for the body.

Have you felt the intimate presence
of Jesus today?

Heaven has a strong pull upon
the soul who calls it home.

Holiness is an unbroken circle.

Holiness is not a solitary life,
but it can be lonely.

Holy Communion means crushing the grain
and the grape and yourself.

Holy living is the proof of repentance.

Holy people are dependent on each other.

How broad is the span of your life's reach?

If your critics throw rocks at you,
save the rocks and build yourself monument.

Ingratitude reveals a selfish spirit.

Is your spiritual vision better
with your eyes open or closed?

It is God's will that our spirit,
soul, and body remain in harmony.

It is possible to hold a doctrine so tight
that it suffocates you.

Life's uncertainties should draw us to God.

Live holy—God is here.

Make hamburger of your sacred cow.

Many would rather harbor in religion
than in principle.

Men are accountable to God for their motives
while mankind judges them by their deeds.

Men would rather appear to be religious by
their words than by their actions.

No one can be neutral with God.

On the physical plane, all are brothers.
On the spiritual level, they may be worlds apart.

Only the pure in heart are holy.

Our worship symbols can
very easily become idols.

Pain to the body may be
pleasure to the soul and spirit.

Some people can clearly hear the whine of
a mosquito but not God's call.

Reality is living today as today,
not as a part of yesterday or tomorrow.

Reject the religion that hardens hearts.

Religious politics is based on social ignorance.

Remember Divinity even when
the danger is past.

Repentance follows confession.
Restitution follows repentance.

Resentment follows spiritual stagnation.

Righteousness is nondenominational.

Some things may be insignificant,
but our attitude toward them
can keep us from heaven.

Spiritual cravings under God's providence
stimulate Christian growth.

Spiritual joys always exceed expectation.

Spiritual stagnation follows resentment.

*The cross reaches from
God's heart to ours.*

The gospel of Jesus turns sacrifice into
privilege and privilege into triumphs.

The Holy Spirit must work in you
before He can work through you.

The knowledge of Jesus is the
grandest truth ever introduced to any person.

*The most potent thought I can have is
that of my responsibility to God.*

The new birth cleanses away
the evil, making a new creation.

The only way to full fellowship with Divinity
is through a heart that is right.

The saint is attracted to things
that draw him to God.

The soul holds the body and spirit together.

The true value of a person is found in his spirit.

The world around you is affected by
the depth of your knowledge of God.

Some religion is like a chicken that
lost its head: very active, but dead.

There is a family resemblance
among God's children.

To be God's friend is
the greatest honor in the universe.

*We carry God's will for
mankind in our hearts.
Few have discovered it.*

We must focus our gaze on Jesus in His
humanity in order to see Him as our example.

We must keep our souls clean so God can
work His will in us.

We need Heavenly Light to walk from
this dark world to the Heavenly City.

What comes to my mind
when I think upon God?

When a person substitutes things for God,
he creates a god.

*When God is in control of my life,
no one else can be.*

When there is no sound,
listen in silence to the communion between
God and your spirit.

When we recognize God's grace,
earthly values dim.

When you come to the end of yourself,
where are you?

Where there is no wonder, no worship occurs.

Where we go for help in times of trouble
reveals our life's motivation.

Without a moral basis, religion is corrupt.

You don't know the strength
of another person's temptation.

Your heart is your soul, and your soul is you.

Your holy life should tell the world
how wonderful Jesus is.

Your soul and spirit can profit from
the body's struggles.

*Your talent came from God.
Use it well.*

SUCCESS

A child's thrill of success in climbing a tree
may be more enduring than
his dad's financial heights.

A successful child usually continues
in the same channel.

**Currency does not determine
true value.**

Enthusiasm promotes success.

Every successful person has dealt with
some bitter disappointment.

Failure is easy to judge—
somehow the definition of success is elusive.

For too many people, success costs too much.

Most failures criticize not themselves
but others' success.

Most of the world strives for survival,
not success.

Success comes not by accident.

Success is amazing. It makes the one who
opposed you wish to be your intimate friend.

*Success is nothing without
being anchored in value.*

Success is usually found
in taking life as it comes.

Success is usually gauged by
those who don't succeed.

Successful people as well as businesses exist
with an eye to the future.

Successful people often start
where others stop.

The jealousy of others is
no measure of success.

*The steps to success may have
very uneven risers.*

The way to glory is usually a plain path.

There are few successes
where there is no opposition.

There are many volunteers to a cause
that has been successfully accomplished.

Today is your vehicle for accomplishment.

Weak-willed men are seldom
useful in great causes.

We make our destinies by choice.

Your dream of success and
God's divine purpose may be opposites.

Suffering

A great disappointment may jolt us
into a better enterprise.

*A heavy heart is fragile.
Carry it prayerfully.*

Adversity and success may be
two sides of the same picture.

Adversity may promote excellence
but receives no credit for its help.

Adversity must be interpreted as
a foreign language.

Adversity reminds men of God.

Adversity teaches more truth
than does prosperity.

All of God's children suffer.

As exercise strengthens the body,
so adversity strengthens the soul.

Be grateful for the safety valve of tears.

Consider the silence of
the long-suffering heart.

Despair is doubt running wild.

Despondency multiplies grief.

Don't be discouraged;
even the sun has its low moments.

Experiencing a period of hard discipline from
God is a form of fasting.

God may allow our hearts to be broken
so that He can get deeper into them.

God uses those people whom He has hurt.

Great characters are usually marked
with heavy scars.

Grief can be a springboard to great thoughts.

Hard times may awaken dormant talents.

*Hardship is God's working
in us to strengthen our souls.*

It is difficult to help a man
who enjoys his troubles.

Joy can be shared; physical pain: never.

*Patience in the face of perplexity
tells of integrity.*

Physical pain eclipses mental suffering.

Physical suffering is pain.
Mental suffering is sorrow.

Please don't give me more troubles;
I don't need the ones I have.

Sorrow and pain reacquaint us
with our humanness.

Sorrow and pain tend to multiply themselves.

The afflicted often give advice
more readily than the prosperous.

The genius usually stays in trouble
while attempting to
help others out of their miseries.

*The grace of God is the
mending glue for broken hearts.*

The greatest deeds are done
by those who suffer.

The only way some people discover truth is
through some adversity.

The person in misery is
silent because it hurts to speak.

The wounded heart has
a greater mandate to do right.

There are many tears in the heart
that don't reach the level of the eyes.

Time has a way of dulling
the sharp point of grief's sword.

Trouble can find its way to your door
even in total darkness.

Trouble is trouble in itself,
but it may lead one to higher experience.

Trouble seems to come at the wrong time.

True strength grows in the face of opposition.

*Where one has suffered for good,
there is holy ground.*

Who pays for a broken heart?

Would it be adversity if we could
understand its cause and purpose?

Would you rather struggle with your own adversity, or seek to relieve the same for another?

Your circumstances are part of a much larger plan.

Your heart and an egg may be the only things that work best when they are broken.

Teaching and Preaching

A poor preacher thinks all preachers are good.

A teacher should have the same craving
for knowledge he expects from his students.

Accepting good counsel is a free education.

An effective teacher opens
doors and windows to truth.

*An ounce of help is better than
a ton of preaching.*

Churches are not to be dormitories,
but armories.

Do you know how to teach someone to live?

Each flower preaches a sermon.

Education is learning to learn.

First teach me with your soul;
then teach me with your words.

Folks learn best while teaching.

In the class you teach,
the most important student is you.

Is what you are teaching worth learning?

It is better for a minister to minister
than for a preacher to preach.

It is hard to take education by faith.

It is often safer to follow a preacher's words
than his life.

Love the preacher who speaks for your good.

More people are proud of their ignorance
than are proud of their learning.

One can teach knowledge,
never wisdom.

One may learn best by teaching a child.

One should teach to learn.

Our will must be educated.

Patience is necessary for teaching children.

Preachers and teachers should
revere their own influence.

Preaching can say much in one word
or nothing in two.

Preaching out of a broken heart
has a healing virtue all its own.

Preaching reminds the hearer of
what he has forgotten.

*Sermons preached from the heart
reach the heart.*

Shouting doesn't make a preacher.

Show me a preacher who says,
"Do as I do, not as I say."

Teachers never complete their learning process.

Teaching teaches the teacher.

The best preaching is done silently.

The good preacher explains.

The great preacher inspires.

The master preacher demonstrates.

The mediocre preacher merely tells.

The preacher should live better than his word.

The preacher who has endured temptation
is most effective.

The properly healthy mind can
teach itself more than seven doctors can.

To effectively learn, teach.

To teach requires a bit of intolerance.

Too many preachers wish to appear
in speech better than they are.

Too much of modern education teaches doubt.

Too often, the sermon
is one thing and
the preacher another.

When some preachers speak,
they sound like cats in canary cages.

TIME

Your view of the future is determined by
your understanding of your past.

As a mortal,
I must deal with eternity as well as time.

Becoming takes a long time.

Both the present and the future are uncertain.

Consider which is the longest:
the past, the present, or the future.

Depression arrives as a black fog dimming the
present with the darkness of the past.

*Don't allow your past failures
to darken future possibilities.*

Everyone's primary counselor is time.

Fear time more than man.

*Few people realize
the power of the present.*

For many people, time is their heaviest load.

I am an accumulation of all my past choices,
good and bad.

If you do the business at hand,
you may see the clearing of the foggy future.

If your past is not properly behind you,
you are walking in the wrong direction.

In thinking of younger days,
we realize the house walls were strong.

Let not the present overpower
the importance of the past and future.

Life is time-consuming.

Many people fondly reflect on past events
that were miserable at the time.

Never reckon time as an adversary;
it will soon win over you.

No matter whom you blame for your past,
you are still responsible for your future.

One second ago is history.

Present misfortunes are
more easily managed than future ones.

Present popularity may have
no effect on future acceptance.

Since there is no constant moment,
each day needs a touch of the future.

The marriage of the past
and the future is the present.

*The one who steals your time
can never repay it.*

The past is a good reflection
but no place to dwell.

The present is time's handle
to carry us into the future.

The reason some people like the good old days
is they were much younger back then.

The word "now" seems to
have a ticking sound.

Time cannot touch the eternal life
within your bosom.

Time consoles.

Time does not choose its enemies.

Time has an insatiable appetite.

Time is always beyond man's power.

Time is always silent; its effects may be noisy.

Time is an unforgiving teacher.

Time is in the middle of eternity.

Time is truth's friend.

To creatively muse on the past
is to chart the future.

Today is God's handle to move us to eternity.

Tomorrow is today's undertaker.

We can sense tomorrow's weaknesses today.

Which causes the most discomfort:
the past, the present, or the future?

While tomorrow seems to be
a daytime occurrence,
it arrives at midnight.

You can return a stolen dollar,
but not a stolen hour.

Your only time is the present.

TROUBLE

A marriage is in trouble when
the husband and wife talk about it.

A tear may be a microscope
focusing on earth's troubles.

Are you grateful for the troubles you have
conquered or for those you have escaped?

Despair: no way out of trouble.

Having more things may mean more troubles.

*Humility prevents
a host of problems.*

If a person talks about his troubles, he may be
working his way out of them.

If I care for you and you care for me,
where is trouble?

Many troubles come as a result of attempting
to defend one's self against a false accusation.

My troubles cannot burden
my heavenly Father.

One way to lessen your troubles is
to look them squarely in the face
and then help other people deal with theirs.

Only he who can deal with trouble
can cope with prosperity.

*Patience is the best remedy
for trouble.*

The lonely person doesn't notice
other people's troubles.

Trouble may lead to higher experience.

Troubles are most often caused by
selfish people.

Troubles come to light at night.

*Troubles pleasantly received
seldom linger.*

When your soul is troubled,
let your mind wander into green colors.

Your troubles give birth to qualities
that nothing else can.

TRUTH

A just cause is never afraid of truth.

A lie can be ninety-nine percent truth.

A shy person may be strong
when truth is threatened.

An argument may reveal
different facets of the same truth.

An atheist
hasn't even a candle of truth to light.

An exaggeration is still a lie.

An open mind attracts truth.

Are the lamps of truth going out?

Belief must yield to truth.

Bruises caused by
the battle for truth often heal slowly.

Cast your life's anchor in truth.

Challenging the future with truth is
the only way to have any effect on it.

Custom is resistant to truth.

Dare to say the truth that others merely think.

Dawning truth is spectacular.

Deceit is always partly true.

Honest discussion winnows truth from error.

Feed your emotions with biblical principles.

Feelings and reason are
only at peace if both are true.

Feelings are never more important than truth.

Feelings are no substitute for truth.

*For truth to last
it must be graven in the heart.*

God put the sand in your life's hourglass.

If you can handle the truth said about you,
certainly the lies should be no problem.

Is truth one of the necessities of your life?

It is better not to touch truth
than to carelessly use it.

It is easier to stand for truth than to act upon it.

*It seems that truth comes to us
rather than our going to it.*

It's sad that in the face of custom,
truth appears a weakling.

Know the truth.

Knowledge is often knowing
where to look for truth.

Let the light of truth shine behind you
to help the lost traveler find the way.

Lies leave scars.

Love the truth.

*Man's wisdom can add nothing
to God's truth.*

Many more martyrs die from an heroic spirit
than from a firm belief in truth.

Much philosophy
refuses to acknowledge truth.

Naked truth causes some to blush.

Never hesitate to go into a battle
when armed with God's truth.

Old beliefs are a major barrier to truth.

One speaks more truth as he grows older.

One who speaks the truth
is often considered radical.

Pity those who
abandon truth in principle's defense.

Preconceived ideas are
often truth's greatest enemy.

Preserve the truth.

Pure doctrine bears pure fruit.

Release the truth.

Search for truth.

Silence can be truth's rapist.

Some approach truth
as a cat toys with a mouse.

Some fear truth because of its absolutes.

Standing alone for truth is true dignity.

Standing on truth makes you tall.

Strict obedience to biblical truths
is a short road to heaven.

Strive to understand truth.

The basis of truth is the fact that God is.

The best part of truth is
that which mere words cannot express.

The divine commandment is to be true.

The history of mankind proves
the truth of the Bible.

The love of truth is the first step to genius.

The most unbelievable thing
for some folks is the truth.

The narrow-minded person
thinks he possesses truth.

The only time some people tell the truth
about themselves is when they are lying.

The response to truth
is often determined by its applicator.

The truth often rests between
one and three inches beneath a lie.

*The wise man states truth
against another person's arguments.*

There is little deliberate lying.
Mostly it is a carelessness about truth.

There is no practicality except in truth.

To many people, truth appears as bad news.

Too many abandon the search for truth.

Too many people guess at the truth.

Truth and good smile at each other.

Truth can be scorched by
the heat of its defenders.

Truth carried in my heart is personalized.

Truth demands action.

Truth does not need
any qualifying explanations.

Truth has its own profound dignity.

Truth has many facets.

Truth has never been popular.

Truth is best expressed in simple words.

Truth is not afraid of open discussion.

Truth is not limited or defined by opinion.

Truth is often sacrificed to opinion or comfort.

Truth is the optimum of life.

Truth is often
the victim in life's battle for right.

Truth makes us accountable.

Truth may anger more people
than it convinces.

Truth may have many humble origins.

Truth needs no defense.

Truth needs no qualifiers.

Truth rises above argument.

Truth rises above reason.

Truth rises above statistics.

Truth sometimes arouses
more controversy than error.

Truth sometimes resembles a briar patch.

Truth spoken by a fool is still truth.

Truth stands.

Truth often stands alone, weeping.

Truth will always win, but the victory may take longer than your lifetime.

Truth will never be rationed.

Truth with a wrong intent is worse than a lie.

What people say behind your back may be true.

Which is easiest to recognize: truth or error?

Why does truth appear an orphan?

Wisdom

A fool and a wise man may do
the same things for different reasons.

A man is happy according to his wisdom.

A new insight into life is a great experience.

A wise man judges his actions beforehand.

A wise person recognizes
the boundary of his ignorance.

*A wise person thinks
before he speaks.*

Accumulated years and multiplied wisdom
prepares one for anything.

An infidel may be a genius,
but only the wise know the Lord.

Are your friends looking to you
for sacred wisdom or for social comfort?

Argument is no proof of wisdom.

Behavior crowns wisdom.

Charm finds friends
while wisdom keeps them.

Cheerfulness is a sign of wisdom.

Don't expect too much from
the instructor's wisdom,
but search with vigor his heart's emotion.

Facts come and go; wisdom tarries.

God in His wisdom has not revealed
all of our abilities to us.

Greet with honor the enthusiastic wise man.

*He who takes advice
is often wiser than he who gives it.*

Hide your wisdom from the foolish man.

Is your wisdom used for public good
or for personal advantage?

It takes a wise person
to believe his own thoughts.

It takes a wise person to know
what to remember and what to forget.

It takes wisdom to know what not to say.

Knowledge of ignorance
is not a sign of wisdom.

Mark that person who has quiet wisdom.

Money cannot speak to the wise person.

Most organizations are operated on
both the wisdom and folly of its members.

Nature and wisdom agree.

*No one can understand
wisdom's light.*

One doesn't need to be
very wise to learn from a fool.

Opinion and feelings
seldom are in contact with wisdom.

Revere those people you know are smart.
Ignore those who think they are.

The enlightened mind
is full of the Light of God's wisdom.

The first step to knowledge
is to recognize wisdom when it appears.

The mind reposes best with wisdom.

The plain man is the real genius.

The wise man is at home anywhere.

The wise person
is not confused about the unknown.

The wise person learns
from every circumstance.

The wise person makes life worth living.

The wise person sees few surprises.

*True wisdom strikes some
like a blinding light.*

Used wisdom is not secondhand.

We should be funnels for wisdom,
not containers.

Wisdom and bigotry are opposites.

Wisdom and honesty are two wheels on a cart.

Wisdom and nature agree.

Wisdom is a high degree of common sense.

Wisdom is determining the difference
between good and evil
and then doing the good.

Wisdom never reaches the point of desperation.

Wisdom outlasts force.

Wisdom usually smiles and seldom frowns.

*Wisdom, like the candle,
must be lit in order to
spread the light.*

You are no wiser than you think.

Your happiness is dependent on your wisdom.

Inspirational Library

Beautiful purse/pocket-size editions of Christian classics bou~
in flexible leatherette. These books make thoughtful gifts f
everyone on your list, including yourself!

When I'm on My Knees The highly popular collection of devotional thoughts on prayer, especially for women.
Flexible Leatherette. $4.97

The Bible Promise Book Over 1,000 promises from God's Word arranged by topic. What does God promise about matters like: Anger, Illness, Jealousy, Love, Money, Old Age, and Mercy? Find out in this book!
Flexible Leatherette. $3.97

Daily Wisdom for Women A daily devotional for women seeking biblical wisdom to apply to their lives. Scripture taken from the New American Standard Version of the Bible.
Flexible Leatherette. $4.97

My Daily Prayer Journal Each page is dated and features a Scripture verse and ample room for you to record your thoughts, prayers, and praises. One page for each day of the year.
Flexible Leatherette. $4.97

Available wherever books are sold.
Or order from:

Barbour Publishing, Inc.
P.O. Box 719
Uhrichsville, OH 44683
http://www.barbourbooks.com

If you order by mail, add $2.00 to your order for shipping.
Prices are subject to change without notice.